FOREST
FOOD WEBS

EARLY BIRD
FOOD WEBS

BY PAUL FLEISHER

LERNER PUBLICATIONS COMPANY • MINNEAPOLIS

The photographs in this book are used with the permission of: © James Randklev/ Photographer's Choice/Getty Images, p. 1; PhotoDisc Royalty Free by Getty Images, pp. 5, 6, 24, 37, 41, 43, 46, 47, 48 (top); © Jason Johnson, p. 7; © Tom Walker/Visuals Unlimited, p. 8; © Tim Hauf/Visuals Unlimited, p. 9; © Gerry Lemmo, pp. 10, 23; © Bill Betty/Visuals Unlimited, pp. 11, 36; © Steve Maslowski/Visuals Unlimited, pp. 12, 26; © Rosemary Calvert/Stone/Getty Images, p. 13; © Scientifica/Visuals Unlimited, p. 14; © SuperStock, Inc./SuperStock, p. 16; © Bill Banaszewski/Visuals Unlimited, p. 17; © Jon Arnold Images/SuperStock, p. 18; © age fotostock/SuperStock, pp. 19, 27; © MedioImages/Getty Images, p. 20; © Fridmar Damm/zefa/CORBIS, p. 21; © Altrendo/Getty Images, p. 22; © Patrick J. Endres/Visuals Unlimited, p. 25; © Joe McDonald/Visuals Unlimited, pp. 28, 30, 31; © Inga Spence/Visuals Unlimited, pp. 29, 42; © Joe McDonald/CORBIS, p. 32; © Gerard Fuehrer/Visuals Unlimited, p. 33; © Fritz Polking/Visuals Unlimited, p. 34; USDA Photo, p. 35; © Dr. Dennis Kunkel/Visuals Unlimited, p. 38; © Getty Images, pp. 39, 40; U.S. Fish and Wildlife Service, p. 48 (bottom). Illustrations on pp. 4, 15 by Zeke Smith, © Lerner Publishing Group, Inc.

Cover: © Scott McKinley/Taxi/Getty Images (top); PhotoDisc Royalty Free by Getty Images (bottom left); © Tom Walker/Visuals Unlimited (bottom right); © James Randklev/Photographer's Choice/Getty Images (background).

Lerner Publications Company
A division of Lerner Publishing Group, Inc.
241 First Avenue North
Minneapolis, MN 55401 U.S.A.

Website address: www.lernerbooks.com

Library of Congress Cataloging-in-Publication Data

Fleisher, Paul.
    Forest food webs / by Paul Fleisher.
        p.   cm. — (Early bird food webs)
    Includes index.
    ISBN: 978-0-8225-6729-5 (lib. bdg. : alk. paper)
    1. Forest ecology—Juvenile literature. 2. Food chains (Ecology)—Juvenile literature. I. Title.
QH541.5.F6F58 2008
577.3—dc22   2007001373

Manufactured in the United States of America
1 2 3 4 5 6 – JR – 13 12 11 10 09 08

CONTENTS

Be A Word Detective .5

Chapter 1
FORESTS .6

Chapter 2
FOREST PLANTS 14

Chapter 3
FOREST PLANT EATERS 22

Chapter 4
FOREST MEAT EATERS 28

Chapter 5
FOREST DECOMPOSERS 34

Chapter 6
PEOPLE AND FORESTS 39

A Note to Adults on Sharing a Book 44

Learn More about Forests and Food Webs 45

Glossary 46

Index 48

A Forest Food Web

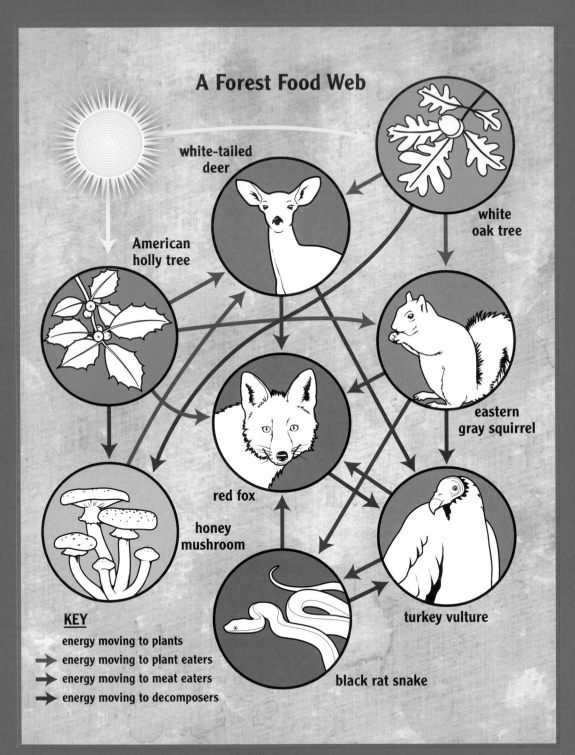

white-tailed deer

white oak tree

American holly tree

eastern gray squirrel

red fox

honey mushroom

turkey vulture

black rat snake

KEY
→ energy moving to plants
→ energy moving to plant eaters
→ energy moving to meat eaters
→ energy moving to decomposers

BE A WORD DETECTIVE

Can you find these words as you read about forest food webs? Be a detective and try to figure out what they mean. You can turn to the glossary on page 46 for help.

bacteria

canopy

carnivores

consumers

decay

decomposers

environments

food chain

food web

herbivores

nutrients

omnivores

photosynthesis

producers

understory

This forest has many tall trees. What other kinds of plants live in forests?

CHAPTER 1
FORESTS

Tall trees tower above you. Fallen leaves cover the ground. Small plants grow in the shade beneath the trees. You are in a forest. Forests are also called woodlands, or woods.

Many different kinds of plants live on the forest floor.

Forests have many trees. They also have bushes, ferns, and mushrooms. Insects and mice live here. So do deer and raccoons. Tiny bacteria (bak-TEER-ee-uh) live in the soil. Bacteria are much too small for us to see.

Forests are some of Earth's most important environments. An environment is the place where any creature lives. The environment includes the air, soil, weather, and other plants and animals.

Red foxes live in forests. Foxes eat other animals. This fox has caught a ground squirrel.

The bump on the ground in this forest is a dead tree. The tree's wood is breaking down. It will become part of the soil.

Plants and animals in the forest depend on one another. Some animals eat living plants. Some creatures eat dead wood and leaves. Other animals are meat eaters. They eat other animals. When plants and animals die, they break down into chemicals (KEH-muh-kuhlz). The chemicals become part of the soil. Some of these chemicals help plants grow.

Energy moves from one living thing to another. A food chain shows how the energy moves. The energy for life comes from the sun. Plants store the sun's energy in their leaves, stems, and roots. When an animal eats a plant, the animal gets some of the sun's energy from the plant. The energy moves farther along the food chain each time one living thing eats another.

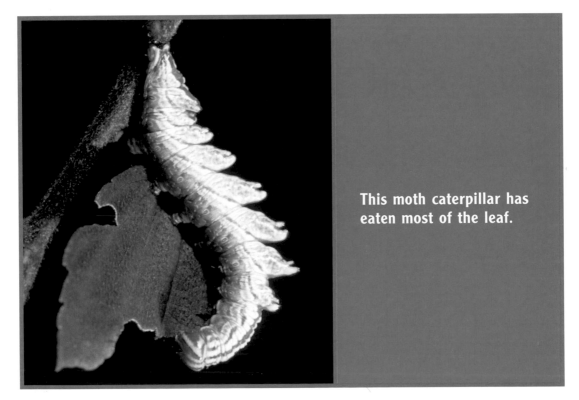

This moth caterpillar has eaten most of the leaf.

A gray catbird is feeding a caterpillar to its babies.

A forest has many food chains. Imagine that a caterpillar eats a leaf. Then a bird eats the caterpillar. A bobcat eats the bird. When the bobcat dies, a vulture eats its body. The sun's energy passes from the leaf to the caterpillar. Then it passes to the bird. Then it goes to the bobcat. Then it goes to the vulture.

This bird is a Swainson's thrush. It is eating a berry. It also eats beetles, ants, caterpillars, and other foods.

But birds don't eat only caterpillars. They also eat seeds, beetles, and worms. Bobcats eat other things besides birds. Bobcats also eat rabbits, squirrels, and mice. And vultures eat all kinds of dead animals. An environment's food web is made up of many food chains. A food web shows how all living things depend on one another for food.

Bobcats eat many kinds of small animals. This bobcat has caught a mouse.

A forest's energy comes from the sun. Plants use sunlight to make food. What else do plants make?

CHAPTER 2
FOREST PLANTS

Green plants use sunlight to make food. Because plants produce food, they are called producers. Plants also make oxygen (AHK-sih-juhn). Oxygen is a gas in the air. All animals need oxygen to breathe.

The way plants make food and oxygen is called photosynthesis (FOH-toh-SIHN-thuh-sihs). Plants need carbon dioxide, sunlight, and water for photosynthesis. Carbon dioxide is a gas in the air. A plant's leaves take in carbon dioxide and sunlight. The plant's roots take in water. The plant uses energy from sunlight to turn the carbon dioxide and water into sugar and starch. Sugar and starch are the plant's own food. The plant stores this food in its leaves and roots.

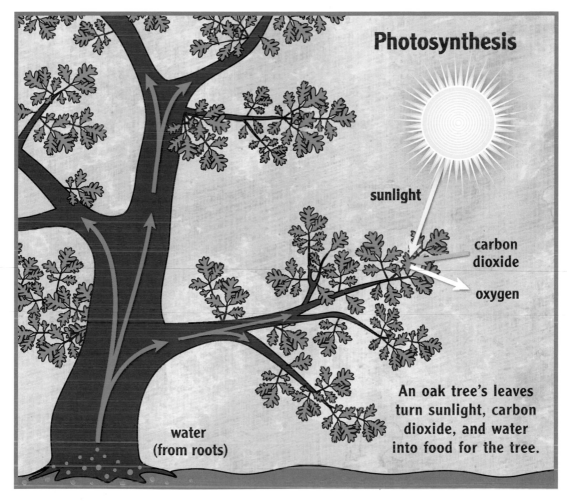

Photosynthesis

sunlight

carbon
dioxide

oxygen

water
(from roots)

An oak tree's leaves turn sunlight, carbon dioxide, and water into food for the tree.

As the plant makes food, it also makes oxygen. The oxygen goes into the air. Animals breathe in the oxygen. They breathe out carbon dioxide. Plants use the carbon dioxide to make more food.

All animals breathe oxygen. This animal is a white-tailed deer.

A tree's roots grow deep into the ground. The roots take in water and nutrients (NOO-tree-uhnts) from the soil.

Plants grow in soil. The soil contains special chemicals called nutrients. Living things need nutrients to grow. When it rains, water soaks into the soil. Nutrients from the soil go into the water. When a plant's roots take in the water, the plant gets nutrients from the soil too. The nutrients become part of the plant.

Trees are the largest plants in a forest. The branches of large trees spread high above the ground. The trees' branches and leaves are called the canopy (KAN-uh-pee). The leaves in the canopy get plenty of sunlight for making food. But the canopy keeps sunlight from reaching the ground.

A forest's canopy blocks most of the light from the sun.

Most saplings grow under older trees.

Young trees are called saplings. Saplings grow on the forest floor. They grow from seeds that fell from older trees. Most saplings die. Many don't get enough light to grow. Others are eaten by animals.

Smaller plants live in forests too. They make up the part of the forest called the understory. Plants in the understory live in the shade of the big trees. But most of these plants don't need much sunlight to live. Blueberry bushes grow in the understory. Mosses, ferns, and flowers grow there too.

Smaller forest plants make up the understory.

Spaces between trees let sunlight reach the ground.

When a big tree dies, it falls down. It leaves an open space in the canopy. The open space is called a clearing. In a clearing, sunlight can reach the forest floor. Saplings can gather a lot of sunlight. They grow quickly. But only a few of them will live long enough to become big trees.

This young porcupine is eating tree bark. What are some other animals that eat plants?

CHAPTER 3
FOREST PLANT EATERS

Animals are called consumers. *Consume* means "eat." Animals that eat plants are called herbivores (ER-buh-vorz). The sun's energy is stored inside plants. When an animal eats a plant, it gets the sun's energy.

Many insects are herbivores. Caterpillars munch on leaves. Leafhoppers suck juices from plants. Bees get their food from flowers.

Some beetles lay eggs under the bark of trees. Grubs hatch from the eggs. Grubs look like short, fat worms. The grubs burrow under the bark. They eat the wood.

The bark has come off of this dead tree. Beetle grubs used to live under the bark. The lines in the wood are tunnels that the grubs made.

Many kinds of birds eat plants. Chickadees
eat seeds. Bluebirds eat berries. Wild turkeys
eat acorns, seeds, and fruit.

Wild turkeys are looking for food in a forest clearing.

This moose is eating the leaves of willow trees.

Mammals are animals with hair that feed their babies milk. Many mammals are herbivores. Mice eat seeds, leaves, roots, and bark. Chipmunks eat nuts and fruit. Deer, moose, and elk are the largest plant eaters in the forest. They munch on leaves and twigs.

Plants can't move around. Many of their seeds fall straight down to the ground. When the seeds sprout, they are in the shade. They don't get enough light to grow well. Animals help to move plants' seeds from place to place.

Nuts are tree seeds. Gray squirrels bury nuts to eat later. But the squirrels forget about some of the nuts. The forgotten nuts may grow into new trees.

Berries have seeds inside them. When a bird eats berries, the seeds pass through its body. When the bird's droppings fall on the ground, the seeds may sprout.

In a different place, the new plants may be able to grow better. Ants and squirrels hide seeds to eat later. Some of the seeds sprout before the animals come back to eat them. When birds eat fruit, seeds from the fruit end up in the birds' droppings. Some of those seeds sprout too.

Toads are meat eaters. This toad is eating an earthworm. What are animals that eat meat called?

CHAPTER 4

FOREST MEAT EATERS

Some forest creatures eat meat. These animals are called carnivores (KAHR-nuh-vorz). Carnivores eat animals. But they need plants too. Carnivores get energy by eating animals that have eaten plants.

28

Spiders are carnivores. Some spiders weave sticky webs. They use the webs to catch flying insects.

This spider has caught a grasshopper.

Rat snakes are good at climbing trees.

Insects can be carnivores too. Wasps capture insects to feed to their young. Ants also hunt and eat other insects.

Toads hide in damp leaves on the forest floor. They hunt earthworms and insects. Black rat snakes climb high into the trees. They search for bird eggs and chicks to eat. They also eat other small animals, such as mice.

Many birds are carnivores. Woodpeckers dig for insects under tree bark. Owls catch mice and rats. Robins eat insects, worms, and other small animals.

Insects live under the bark of this tree. The woodpecker is using its long tongue to eat the insects.

Many mammals are carnivores too. Foxes eat mice, birds, and snakes. Opossums eat insects, rabbits, and worms.

Opossums hunt small animals such as insects and worms. But they also eat meat from animals that have already died. This opossum is eating a rabbit.

Black bears eat both animals and plants. This bear is eating fruit from a crab apple tree.

Some animals eat both plants and meat. These animals are called omnivores (AHM-nuh-vorz). Raccoons eat frogs, snakes, birds, small mammals, nuts, and fruit. Bears are the largest omnivores in the forest. They eat deer, fish, insects, roots, and berries.

This dead tree has fallen down. Many dead trees fall down every year. Why isn't the ground covered with dead trees?

CHAPTER 5
FOREST DECOMPOSERS

All living things die. When plants and animals die, they decay. They break down into nutrients. Living things called decomposers help dead things decay. Decomposers feed on dead plants and animals.

Decomposers are nature's recyclers. They break down dead plants and animals. Nutrients from the dead plants and animals go into the soil. Then other living things can use the nutrients.

Decomposers are very important. Without them, forests would be filled with dead plants and animals. Then no new plants could grow. Animals would run out of food.

Tiny bacteria are breaking down these dead leaves. Nutrients from the leaves will go into the soil.

Pill bugs are also called sow bugs or wood lice.

Many insects are decomposers. Termites
live in the wood of dead trees. They eat the
wood. They slowly turn the trees into soil.
Some beetles and flies lay their eggs on dead
animals. When the young insects hatch, they
feed on the dead bodies.

Beetles and pill bugs hide under rotting
logs. They eat dead wood and leaves.

Earthworms burrow deep into the soil. They feed on rotting leaves.

Mushrooms and other fungi (FUHN-jye) are decomposers too. Fungi get their food from dead leaves and wood. Many different kinds of fungi live in forests.

Fungi are growing on a rotting log.

Bacteria also feed on dead plants and animals. Bacteria are all around us. But they are so tiny we cannot see them.

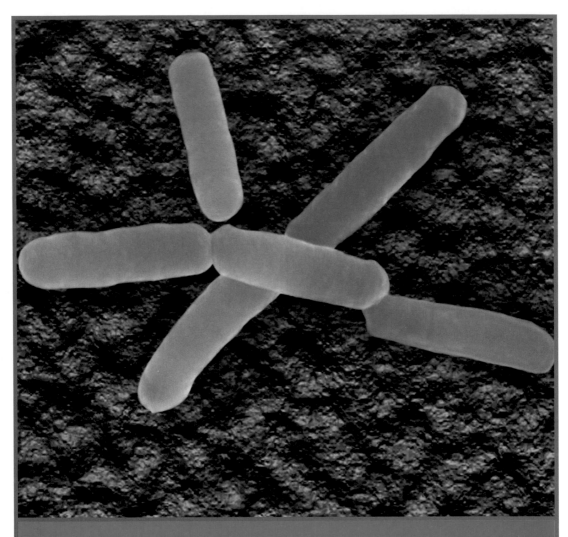

There are many kinds of bacteria. They live nearly everywhere on Earth. This picture shows one kind of bacteria that lives in soil.

This family is walking through a forest. Why do people like to visit forests?

CHAPTER 6
PEOPLE AND FORESTS

Many people like to visit forests. People hike and camp in the woods. They enjoy watching forest animals and sitting under shady trees.

Part of this forest was cut down. People have planted new trees. The trees will take a long time to grow tall.

People use forests for other things too. People cut down trees. They use wood from the trees to build houses. They also make wood into paper. This book was once a tree growing in a forest.

After trees are cut down, new trees grow. But trees grow slowly. It takes many years for a forest to grow. When a forest's trees are cut down, animals that lived in the trees must find new homes.

Plants need soil to grow. Trees keep the soil from washing away during heavy rains. The leaves of trees keep raindrops from pounding against the ground. Trees' roots hold the soil in place. When a forest is cut down, heavy rain may carry away the soil.

This place was once a forest. People cut down most of the trees. Rain has washed away a lot of the soil.

Sometimes fires start in forests. A fire may start when lightning strikes a tree. People cause forest fires too. They may be careless with matches. Or they may forget to put out a campfire. Fire can help a forest. It burns away dead leaves and fallen branches. It makes room for new plants to grow. But fire is harmful too. Forest fires destroy many trees and other plants. They kill woodland animals.

A fire burned down many trees in this forest. But new trees have sprouted. Very slowly, the forest is growing back.

Forests are home to many different kinds of plants and animals.

Much of the United States was once covered with forests. But people cut down many trees to make space for cities and farms. We have to protect the woodlands that are left. Forests are important to people. And they are important to the plants and animals that live in them.

ON SHARING A BOOK

When you share a book with a child, you show that reading is important. To get the most out of the experience, read in a comfortable, quiet place. Turn off the television and limit other distractions, such as telephone calls. Be prepared to start slowly. Take turns reading parts of this book. Stop occasionally and discuss what you're reading. Talk about the photographs. If the child begins to lose interest, stop reading. When you pick up the book again, revisit the parts you have already read.

BE A VOCABULARY DETECTIVE

The word list on page 5 contains words that are important in understanding the topic of this book. Be word detectives and search for the words as you read the book together. Talk about what the words mean and how they are used in the sentence. Do any of these words have more than one meaning? You will find the words defined in a glossary on page 46.

WHAT ABOUT QUESTIONS?

Use questions to make sure the child understands the information in this book. Here are some suggestions:

What did this paragraph tell us? What does this picture show? What is a food web? How do plants depend on animals? Where does a forest's energy come from? What do we call animals that eat both plants and animals? How do fires help forests? What is your favorite part of the book? Why?

If the child has questions, don't hesitate to respond with questions of your own, such as What do *you* think? Why? What is it that you don't know? If the child can't remember certain facts, turn to the index.

INTRODUCING THE INDEX

The index helps readers find information without searching through the whole book. Turn to the index on page 48. Choose an entry such as *plants* and ask the child to use the index to find out how plants make their own food. Repeat with as many entries as you like. Ask the child to point out the differences between an index and a glossary. (The index helps readers find information, while the glossary tells readers what words mean.)

FORESTS AND FOOD WEBS

BOOKS

Bishop, Nic. *Forest Explorer: A Life-Size Field Guide.* New York: Scholastic, 2004.

Capeci, Anne. *Food Chain Frenzy.* New York: Scholastic, 2003.

Johnson, Rebecca L. *A Walk in the Boreal Forest.* Minneapolis: Lerner Publications Company, 2001.

Johnson, Rebecca L. *A Walk in the Deciduous Forest.* Minneapolis: Lerner Publications Company, 2001.

Johnson, Rebecca L. *A Walk in the Rain Forest.* Minneapolis: Lerner Publications Company, 2001.

Riley, Peter. *Food Chains.* New York: Franklin Watts, 1998.

WEBSITES

All About Rainforests
http://www.enchantedlearning.com/subjects/rainforest/
This colorful site has information on some of the plants and animals that live in rain forests, plus quizzes, activities, and more.

Chain Reaction
http://www.ecokids.ca/pub/eco_info/topics/frogs/chain_reaction/index.cfm#
Create a food chain and find out what happens if one link is taken out of the chain.

Food Chains and Webs
http://www.vtaide.com/png/foodchains.htm
This website has an interactive tool to let you create your own food webs.

Smokey Kids
http://www.smokeybear.com/kids/
This Web page has forest facts, information on forest fires, games, and more.

GLOSSARY

bacteria (bak-TEER-ee-uh): tiny living things made up of just one cell. Bacteria can be seen only under a microscope.

canopy (KAN-uh-pee): the branches and leaves of the large trees in a forest

carnivores (KAHR-nuh-vorz): animals that eat meat

consumers: living things that eat other living things. Animals are consumers.

decay: to break down

decomposers: living things that feed on dead plants and animals

environments: places where creatures live. An environment includes the air, soil, weather, plants, and animals in a place.

food chain: the way energy moves from the sun to a plant, then to a plant eater, then to a meat eater, and finally to a decomposer

food web: many food chains connected together. A food web shows how all living things in a place need one another for food.

herbivores (ER-buh-vorz): animals that eat plants

nutrients (NOO-tree-uhnts): chemicals that living things need in order to grow

omnivores (AHM nuh vorz): animals that eat both plants and meat

photosynthesis (FOH-toh-SIHN-thuh-sihs): the way green plants use energy from sunlight to make their own food out of carbon dioxide and water

producers: living things that make their own food. Plants are producers.

understory: the small trees, bushes, and other plants that live under the tall trees in a forest

INDEX

Pages listed in **bold** type refer to photographs.

decomposers, 9, 32, 34–38

energy moving through a forest,
    10–11, **14**, 22, 28

fires, 42
food chains and food webs, 11–13

meat eaters, 9, **11**, **12**, **13**, 28–33

omnivores, 33

people and forests, 39–40, 42–43
plant eaters, **8**, 9, **10**, **12**, 22–27
plants, 6–7, 14–21

soil, 9, 17, **35**, **38**, 41

trees, 6, 18–19, 21, **26**, **34**, 40–41, **42**